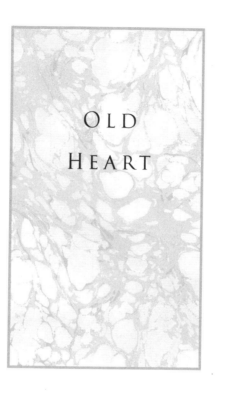

OLD

HEART

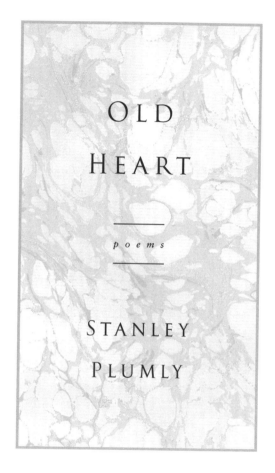

OLD
HEART

poems

STANLEY
PLUMLY

W. W. Norton & Company   New York   London

For information about permission to reproduce selections from this book,
write to Permissions, W. W. Norton & Company, Inc.,
500 Fifth Avenue, New York, NY 10110

For information about special discounts for bulk purchases, please contact
W. W. Norton Special Sales at
specialsales@wwnorton.com or 800-233-4830.

Manufacturing by Courier Westford
Book design by Chris Welch
Production manager: Julia Druskin

Library of Congress Cataloging-in-Publication Data

Plumly, Stanley.
Old heart : poems / Stanley Plumly.—1st ed.
p. cm.
ISBN 978-0-393-06568-8 (hardcover)
I. Title.
PS3566.L78O43 2007
811'.54—dc22

2007014827

W. W. Norton & Company, Inc.
500 Fifth Avenue, New York, N.Y. 10110
www.wwnorton.com

W. W. Norton & Company Ltd.
Castle House, 75/76 Wells Street, W1T 3QT

1 2 3 4 5 6 7 8 9 0

A C K N O W L E D G M E N T S

Thanks are due the editors of the following magazines in which poems in this volume were originally published, many of which have undergone—sometimes radical—revision: *AGNI*, *The American Poetry Review*, *The Atlantic Monthly*, *Blackbird*, *Conjunctions*, *DoubleTake*, *Field*, *Hotel Amerika*, *The Georgia Review*, *The Gettysburg Review*, *The Greensboro Review*, *The Green Mountains Review*, *The Harvard Review*, *The Kenyon Review*, *The Nation*, *The New Republic*, *The New Yorker*, *Poetry*, *Poetry Northwest*, *Ploughshares*, *32 Poems*, *Threepenny Review*, *TriQuarterly*, *The Valparaiso Review*, *The Yale Review*.

"Greensboro Campus Sonnet," "Nostalgia," "Samuel Scott's *A Sunset, with a View of Nine Elms*," and "Still Missing the Jays" appeared in the chapbook, *Nostalgia* (Zumbro River Press, 2003).

Special thanks to Megan Riley in the preparation of this book. The epigraph is from act 4, scene 1, *Henry V*.

FOR DAVID BAKER

God-a-mercy, old heart, thou speak'st cheerfully.

CONTENTS

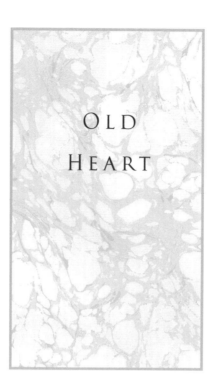

OLD
HEART

BUTTERFLIES

Inevitably alchemy, the lesser into the greater,
morphing to the pupa stage, the chrysalis,
but faster, the cuticle of skin sloughed off,
regrown, and shed again, each larval, instar
meta phase passing through more molting lives
than saints—five, six times before the final birth,
then into the light, like eyes wadded up, then slowly,
with the blood, wings opening. Opening and closing.
For those that fly like birds, at least four inches
tip to wingtip, continent to continent, Emperors,
Monarchs, Giant Swallowtails, large enough to feed
like leaves along the branches or be the blown leaf
drinking from the dung pool hoofprint in the mud—
size the compensation and camouflage for color.
For those that fly the garden, in graduated light,
like those that live inside us, smaller, different
distances, in colors just arrived at by pigment
or reflection, tiny scales of forewings and hindwings
overlapping, colors the secret shadings of the sun—
dawn yellows, blood oranges, fritillary reds, gentian
blues, each slighter than a whistle blade, like
hummingbirds seen through, Flame Coppers, Streak
Indigos, White Bruise, intensity at once-in-a-
lifetime brightness, Brightness at the flower
finding food, inside the maul and marl of the mouth—

SPIRIT BIRDS

The spirit world the negative of this one,
soft outlines of soft whites against soft darks,
someone crossing Broadway at Cathedral, walking
toward the god taking the picture, but now,
inside the camera, suddenly still. Or the spirit
world the detail through the window, manifest
if stared at long enough, the shapes of this
or that, the lights left on, the lights turned off,
the spirits under arcs of sycamores the gray-gold
mists of migratory birds and spotted leaves recognize.

Autumnal evening chill, knife edges of the avenues,
wind kicking up newspaper off the street,
those ghost peripheral moments you catch yourself
beside yourself going down a stair or through
a door—the spirit world surprising: those birds,
for instance, bursting from the trees and turning
into shadow, then nothing, like spirit birds
called back to life from memory or a book,
those shadows in my hands I held, surprised.
I found them interspersed among the posthumous pages

of a friend, some hundreds of saved poems: dun
sparrows and a few lyrical wrens in photocopied
profile perched in air, focused on an abstract
abrupt edge. Blurred, their natural color bled,
they'd passed from one world to another: the poems,
too, sung in the twilit middle of the night, loved,
half-typed, half-written-over, flawed, images
of images. He'd kept them to forget them.
And every twenty pages, in xerox ash-and-frost,
Gray Eastern, Gold Western, ranging across borders.

MERCY

A murder of crows,
what I saw on a spindle of dead white oak,
two or three of them, at different times,
hectoring the head of the sick one,
the old one, the weak one apart.
From school those Eskimo stories
in which leathery grandfathers and grandmothers
are left behind or set afloat.
They'd freeze, Mr. Steinman said, from the extremities in.
Thinking about what they must have been thinking,
I imagined the brain last
on the ascending list—
As Freezing persons, recollect the Snow
I read, in chilling poetry,
years later. Even at twelve,
the concept seemed distant, efficient,
in keeping with the clarity
and killing cold of vast, undifferentiated arctic spaces.
In keeping with the landscape of the old.
In the language of the desert Navajo,
the old man didn't drown,
the water came up to get him.
That's how I imagined freezing,
as a kind of incremental drowning,
a sort of slow, word by word submersion,
then, at last, the pulling under, rings on water.

The killed crow fell the sixty feet in seconds,
less, though in the while it took
to find it, it had moved. My mother,
alive in the machine,
becalmed on hard white sheets,
the narrative of legs, arms,
animal centers stilled,
some starlight in the mind glittering off
and on, couldn't tell me
whether or not to leave her.

ELEVENS

1

The sun flatlining the horizon, the wind
off the Atlantic hard enough to swallow—
arctic, manic, and first thing—
the morning beach walk north lasting less
than half an hour, while you've stood
in the middle of the room that long
trying to get your breath back to normal.
It seems to take all the time there is,
as if a flake of ash burning off the sun
had entered at the mouth, turned ice,
and had, in slow-borne seconds, grown

2

glacial, granite, dark. The summer
in the mountains there was snow, new snow,
you could walk in fifteen minutes down
the narrow gravel road and there'd be
ghostweed, spiraea, and stunted laurel trees
blossoming their own snow-on-the-mountain.
Ten, eleven thousand feet, and the water,
with a spirit of its own, moving over rock
without once touching, flying toward the world.
The thin fresh air too spiritual as well.
Down below, with lights, Durango, Colorado.

3

City snow, especially, transforms backwards—
antique, baroque, medieval, hand-to-mouth.
Karel Čapek, in a book called *Intimate
Things*, says Prague can go back one, two
hundred years just overnight in a three-
or four-inch snowfall, as in the stillness
of a postcard of the Charles, looking from
the square in Mala Strana toward the sad-faced
saints along the high sides of the bridge,
snow-capped, blessed and even fouled with
the Old World and other-worldly, since Prague

4

is a winter city, night city, streetlights
blurred in mist, the centuries-looming
buildings basic gothic under the glow.
Čapek adds "that you are startled at the
darkness deep within you" standing in
the history and cold beauty of the place.
Kundera, too, clarifies the quality of light,
as if among the weight of intimate things
you were lifted, and the face in the water
looking up from the river were not yours,
and those weren't your footprints in the snow.

5

Water filling a void created by a glacier—
hundreds of these lakes healing over wounds.
And when you choose you must be silent.
So we'd row out slowly, barely lifting up
our oars, in order to fool the fish, who'd
rise to see what foolish fish we were, then
go back down. Fresh water, black water deep.
You had the sense, at dusk, of dreaming,
of floating in a light now almost gone—
the anchor tied to a ladder, oars like wings,
but nowhere to go but drifting until morning.

6

At a height above Punto Spartivento,
the point at which the northern wind divides,
Como and Lecco assume their separate waters,
deep enough they've drained the deepest sky.
The lift from the lakes' sun surfaces is
swallows, terns, and Mediterranean gulls,
green hills and granite mountains, white
tourist boats and seaplanes circling in, then
steps beyond the timed arrivals and departures,
terraces and gardens of terra-cotta towns
that look like, from here, no one lives there.

7

Eliot says that home is where you start from,
memory and body so confused they are the same.
In London, in Holland Park, in late October
on a Sunday, in an after-rain late afternoon,
I stood under the great horse chestnut
I'd stood under in the spring when it lit
its candelabra into flame. The chestnuts,
like the eyes of deer, were gone—buckeyes
if you'd grown up in Ohio, conkers if you
played them or fed them to the horses.
And half the leaves were gone. Yet through

8

the intricate yellow lattice of what was left
the changing sky took on a shape less random.
Eliot, in "East Coker," also says that as we
grow older the world becomes stranger, the sky,
the painter's sky, transformative as earth—
Constable's woolgathering, towering clouds,
Turner's visceral, annihilating sunsets.
I went to this tree every season for a year.
In winter it was purity, in summer full green
fire. The sky's huge island canopy felt focused
through its branching, the ground more certain.

9

The way a child might hide. I remember walking
into the sharp high grass of a hay field, lying
down, closing my eyes. If you were patient
with the insects and the paper cuts of blades
you could, after a while, hear the Moloch
under earth, and in your mind, if you tried,
ascend into the afterlife of air hovering
just above you. It had to be that falling
time of day the sun is level with the dead last
word. Levitation was the first word you thought
of down on a knee in the hospital, kissed. . . .

10

When I saw my heart lit up on the screen,
the arteries, veins, and ventricles
all functioning, pictured, as if removed,
in picture-space, I knew that this is
what is meant by distance, the way, flying
once at forty thousand feet, the needle nose
of the needle flashing in the sun, traveling
alone, and nothing but clarity under us,
I felt like a visitor inside my own body.
I could see myself invisible on the ground
following the threadbare vapor trail. We

11

claim the body as a temple or cathedral,
meaning the house in which I am that I am,
blood and bone, water, mortar, breath.
Brunelleschi, bricking up the eggshell
of his dome, understood the soul must live
in space constructed out of nature.
He could see within his double-vaulted,
self-supporting ceiling a sky "higher
than the sky itself." When I was there,
in the Duomo, looking up, the terror of
a bird took all the heart out of the air.

MAGPIE

First, the fence-sitting, followed by
the preening in a pool of early rain,
looking like he's looking at himself,
the air a kind of looking glass as well.
Yesterday, on the small plane coming in
over the rise and fall of the Santa Rosas,
half the crowded flight shutting down
their laptops, and later, on the ground,
starting up their cellphones, talking
money, talking time, talking love, talking
the whole ride from the airport through
fluent empty avenues garden paced
with palms and acreage of rows of beds
of cyclamen and California poppies. . . .
Yesterday that seems a week ago—.

                    Now
here, at the Riviera,
a middling stop shoe-horned between
the old wealth and the new, the flowering
jacarandas are also on display,
their lavender-lit pale blossoms,
like their bell-shaped inflorescence,
a delicate extravagance: though
the gardener, a native of their native
tropic source, is proud of their elegance

and the elegant fern-like shade they throw
from fifty feet. *Brazil*, he says,
in Anglo-Portuguese, pronouncing *jaca-
randa* as if it were a dance, something
to sing.

                  The bluing sky is something lyric, too,
after the rain and thinning desert wind,
water gathering the summer in the mountains.
Look for the herons, the gardener says,
and sure enough last night they flew
just overhead, white as wedding gloves.
Doubtless tomorrow we'll play a middling
tennis, then a long swim on surfaces
like mirrors. Rich man's, poor man's body.
Meanwhile, Blue-Black-and-White, assembled,
is lifting from his pool,
in a tux with tails—
scapulars, wing patches, and shirt front
showing—and if he lands in a jacaranda
that will be something.

MISSING THE JAYS

What's missing, morning after morning,
are their shrill, swift barkings-down,
their *shkrrring* blue-flight strike alarms—
or later, from the thawing underbrush,
the clicking metered phrases Emily
Dickinson calls civic in felicity.
Blue breaking the gray-white-black
of stillness, habits of silence—
what's missing are their fierce
collective tempers.

              And all of them,
not just one male militant inter-
changeable malcontent, one bluer
or louder, one stronger, one faster,
but all of them now missing as if they'd
disappeared, their hectoring mob
predatory selves left to their cousins,
crows, their beauty to the cardinals,
brighter than blood in the veins
of red maples.

By spring the sky will darken
with all the usual birds lining the wires
and walls, divining their survival
(bird-in-the-hand-sized sparrows,
brackish English starlings, feral
mongrel doves), when what'll be missing
in the corner of the eye the second
the head is turned is blue—jay blue—
and then the moment gone, and the *jaaay*
jaaay sound, like a jeer, gone with it.

STILL MISSING THE JAYS

Then this afternoon in the anonymous winter hedge I saw one.
I'd just climbed, in my sixty-year-old body—
with its heart attacks, kidney stones,
torn Achilles tendon, vague promises of ulcers,
various subtle, several visible permanent scars,
ghost-gray hair, long nights and longer silences,
impotence and liver spots, evident translucence,
sometime short-term memory loss—
I'd just climbed out of the car
and there it was, eye-level, looking at me,
young, bare blue,
the crest and marking jewelry penciled in,
smaller than it would be if it lasted
but large enough to show the dark adult
and make its queedle and complaint.
It seemed to wait for me, watching
in that superciliary way birds watch, too.
So I took it as a sign, part spring, part survival.
I hadn't seen a jay in years—
I'd almost forgotten they existed.
Such obvious, quarrelsome, vivid birds
that turn the air around them crystalline.
Such crows, such ravens, such magpies!
Such bristling in the spyglass of the sun.

Yet this one, new in the world,
softer, plainer, curious.
I tried to match its patience, not to move,
though when it disappeared to higher ground
I had the thought that if I opened up my hand—

DEBT

Pound, for whom collateral was metaphor,
Stevens, for whom poetry was a kind of money,
Eliot, who counted money in a bank—O
let them be the three or four dour men
standing around the outside of the house
funereally in overcoats, stamping their feet,
staring or looking down, faintly breathing

fire. It's a hard Ohio morning, snowing.
My father's out there, too, in shirtsleeves,
hands in his pockets, two or three tired years
past thirty. Then one of the men is writing
in a book that makes me think of school,
the others drawing pictures in the air,
which is the still gray grainy white of paper.

What else: except they measure off the fencerows,
walk the acre frontage, wade a sort of circle
of the house as if they're going to buy it.
What else: except the window ice and cold
and hole enough to see through: secrecy, fell
silence, and intermittent, fragmentary snow,
fields of it, and half a mile or less the B & O.

Pound defined usury as the tax on borrowed time
by those who own mortality. I wish Pound
had been there. I wish someone like him.
He had the moment's right mad temperament
and the animal face of the prophet. Wallace
Stevens as well in that grave wool worsted
coat he wore on his wintry walks to work. The w's

like angels in the snow. The greatest poverty,
he said, is not to live within a physical world.
Great poverty is what it felt like when they
stood like winter itself in the middle
of the room talking figures. I was nine
or ten and twenty years from poetry, when Eliot
said imagination is different from fulfillment.

CHILDHOOD

You couldn't keep it out. You could see it
drifting from one side of the road to the other,
watch the wind work it back and forth across
the hard white surfaces, then the oak,
with its ten dead leaves, winded, wanting it.
But you couldn't keep it out.
It was like dust, an elegance, like frost. . . .
All you had to do was stand at the window
and it passed like the light over your face,
softer than light, at the edges, the seams,
the separations in the glass. All you had to do
was stand still in the dark and the room
seemed alive with it, a bright breath on the air.
If you fell asleep you knew it could cover you,
the way cold closes on water. It could shine,
like ice, inside you. And if you woke up early,
the cup on the bureau cracked, you were sure
that even pockets of your pants would be filled.
Nothing could stop it, could keep it out,
not the room in sunlight nor neutral
like the rain, not the sweeper sweeping
nor the builder building woodfires each morning,
not the wind blowing backwards without sound. . . .

•

Where the sky seems to separate the clouds,
the clouds the sky, the white oaks all lean in
on one another, snowy, hollow, still gothic
with winter. And the few torn leaves
starved natural back into the spring before
this one, the one long since gone black
under the ice, hold on, mark time. . . .
They'll drop eventually once, twice, and turn
bright green again blossoming. And the few
songbirds, stationed out of sight in the high
cold crowns, barely audible, almost mythical. . . .
They'll sing true again, fly, and fall to earth
awhile. And this is promised, too, that
the wind left trapped in the blue alleys
of the branches will calm and clarify
in the risen, rising air. Let the stone gods
in their fountains move like clockwork—
they're no less rooted in the rain
nor their marble less perfection of the snow—
let the clay gods circle in the fire. The body
piecemeal wastes away, the something soul
slips from the mouth, muse and sacred memory
shuts its eyes. I died, I climbed a tree, I sang.

KEATSIAN

My brand-new Schwinn, its narrow English wheel.
I'd turn and circle figure eights until
I couldn't see or fell, the deep sun lost
behind the trees. I was as tall as Keats.
The game was numbers or the alphabet.
Later sorts of sonnets, quatrains, couplets.
Nobody died, as someone's mother or
mother-in-law would say about divorce.
At the end, sailing to south Italy,
grown-up Keats writes Brown that while "Land and Sea,
weakness and decline are . . . seperators . . .
death is the great divorcer forever."
In his marriage of the poem to matter,
written in stone if written in water.

SIMILE

This heart I found at lowtide this morning,
accurate to a fault, hand-sized, heart-shaped,
with the thick weight of a heart, a perfect
piece of limestone cut by hand by the sea
who knows how long, brought up from the bottom
again and again, split like our own hearts,
nicked from the top half down, as if in another
life it had been real, stone atrium, stone sorrow,
stone ventricles, stone arteries and veins.

And these glittering halves of oyster shells
I picked this afternoon, like the stones
worn into shape, swirled, half-eaten-out, still
oiled and pearly-wet, with edges sharp enough
to clean a fish. Imagine that the oysters
have survived, like eyes of the otherworldly
or symbols of some sexual potency, look-alikes
for testicles or a woman's soft insides,
as we drink them down by swallowing them whole. . . .

In the doctrine of signatures things become
themselves as something else, as we are who
we are word of mouth. Then I found a bird,
a kind of gull, eaten by the fish and other birds,
one missing wing, one eye, the rest of it
so rendered past resemblance you throw it back,

into the void, the chaos it came from,
yet the moment it goes under it's a memory,
a metaphor, we say, for what we can't quite

name, tip of the tongue, whistle in the bone,
death in its variety, its part-by-piece detail.
Like the skull washed up one lost-and-found
new year, fallen from the ocean sky,
dead off the moon, something to conjure with,
now set on the desk on the bony back of its head,
neither human nor animal but brilliant white
brain-coral, pitted, scalloped, furrowed
at the brow, its stone, teardrop-shaped face

a mask for mourning. Unlike the shapely clouds,
changeable, emotional, a skein of moving mare's
tails, a skimmer's broken wing, cumulonimbus
palaces where once-and-future beings act out
their human longing. I went down to the sea,
the source of life, it was filled to overflowing.
The blue horizon line, however many miles,
parted nothing more than air from bluer water,
though it was poetry to say what it looked like.

PARAPHRASE OF THE PARABLE OF THE PRODIGAL SON

A certain man has two sons,
as a king may have three daughters.
The younger of his sons says to the father,
give me the portion of goods that falls to me.
The youngest daughter will say to her father,
I love you in a portion that cannot be measured in goods.
And the father-king, if he is old,
may confuse, through pride, her meaning.
The father of the two sons divides his living between them,
with the result that the younger gathers all together
and takes a journey to a far country
where he wastes his substance with riotous living.
Her sisters, taking advantage of their father's confusion,
may claim to love him without qualification of his living.
There arises a famine in that far land
and the younger son begins to be in want,
so much so that he takes up with the swine
of the herd he is tending and eats as they eat.
A king may punish an ungrateful child,
send her into exile into a far country.
He may deprive her of all his goods.
He may dote on her sisters.
At last the son comes to his senses
and returns home to his father's fields,
knowing he has sinned: Father, he will say, I am no more
worthy to be called your son, make me as one of your servants.

But as the father sees him coming yet a great way off
he has compassion and runs to greet his prodigal son.
Bring forth the best robe and rings and shoes,
he instructs the servants, let us kill the fatted calf,
for this my son was dead, and is alive again,
he was lost and is found. The lost sister may not be found.
The king, like old Saturn, will be blind
to what surrounds him. He is a tragic figure,
and thus his true daughter must suffer her father.
A king will punish an ungrateful child. The elder son,
working in the fields, hears the music of the meal,
and goes and stands outside the house demanding explanation.
Lo, these many years have I served you and your commandments,
yet you never killed for me the fatted calf.
My brother wastes his goods on harlots,
and for him you make a feast. Son, says the father,
you are always with me, all that I have is yours.
But it was meet that we should feast and be glad.
Your brother was dead and is alive again.
The king, however, cannot bring back his daughter,
nor any of the family he has broken. He will die,
like many of us, without children.

MEETING MR. COLE

I remember I sat in the backseat with a tire
and fishing paraphernalia and an open rusty
toolbox, as if this part of the car (a sea-salt
scoured blue Chevy) were part of the trunk,
the whole rear end so roadbound it meant
the shocks were gone. Henri's father,
a former Navy man ("Stars on his blue serge
uniform flaunt a feeling"), just fit
the driver's seat, navigating flawlessly
the floating high front end through close
suburban waters. He was tall, like Henri,
but utterly, apparently, opposite from Henri's
natural elegance, work hands on the wheel,
white beard, his light eyes rinsed out red
in heavy glasses, his militant sailor's face
too used to the sun, the look I saw myself in
in the future. The way I remember my father's
welder's face boiled above me when he held me
by the wrists over a fire or what felt like one.
Henri's father was that softer soul, a fisherman,
a beach bum, someone who'd retired early deeply.
Whether he met us or took us to the station
at New Carrollton I've forgotten (we'd commute
from Boston and Manhattan south to teach),
and why this particular trip he was there
to greet his son I'm not sure, this mariner

out too far too many years. What mattered was
the moment. So you had to be struck by
the anger yet affection between them,
the absences and silences (the father's
eventual ashes in a cup), then the caring, shy
formalities; struck by how similar yet different
they seemed, how we all change with time but don't.

THE TREASON OF TERESE SVOBODA

He'd be a graduate student now, as you were.
He was a kind of student then,
studying at your breast, carried there
or softly on your back.
Sometimes, if we couldn't find a sitter
during class, he'd join us, speak his mind.
He was, like every child, palpable.
Your book arrived today, your eighth,
and, as always, preoccupied with edges,
but this time less angry, more tender.
Many of the poems "circle,"
as the jacket copy says,
"the subject of the mother as betrayer,
creator and destroyer." They circle it,
I suppose, in order to contain it,
the way you circled,
in those difficult young years,
the road map of the world in exile.
The title poem states "It takes
three for treason . . . / Three. Two to begat one."
And in the last poem, "Bacchae," these
impossible lines: "When she hears him fall, /
she runs to catch him—/
but you cannot both birth and catch."
He was sitting looking down from a high open window.
I don't remember, twenty-five years later,

how he got there. Perhaps you wanted him
to breathe the better air above the city.
Perhaps you wanted him to see.
Perhaps he got there on his own.
The cover on your book is "full of eyes,"
from a painting by a woman in 1942,
who may or may not have been a mother,
but who knows what accusation is,
the power of being seen.
Your hair in your picture is the sheer lit
white of the afterlife, the sheen
of clouds in heaven we imagine.
I think of you alone, rushing to the window, looking down.

PANEGYRIC FOR THE PLANE TREE FALLEN ON FIFTH AVENUE

At the end of Eighty-eighth,
across from the museum and as west as east
will take you to the park from Gracie Mansion.
Before the lightning brought it down,
before it fell at evening rush hour,
before another summer burned the money
off its leaves, before
it put a sudden stop to double lanes of traffic,
you could stand here late at night
in the middle of the street
and watch it grow,
the outer darker skin
flaking to the bone bark underneath.
It was probably too tall,
and filled too easily with wind,
too brilliantly with rain
and ice and snow.
And probably its roots were shallow
with the sidewalk, the breakable
high branches threatening.
Maybe it was thirty, thirty-five years old,
planted in the forties, after war,
and because of where it was,
flowering like a blessing,
allowed its larger seasons.
In 1979, sempiternal and a year,

the city was a buyer's market,
if you already owned
and had a million in the bank.
Mornings the gold coin of the sun
rose from the East River, set in the Hudson.
These hybrids of the sycamore
lined all the avenue along the park.
If a tree falls in the forest . . .
If a tree has no witness . . .
A hundred of us saw it hit and fall.
Fall slow enough no one near was caught.
First the thunderbolt thrown straight
at its carved heart, then
the killing blood-spurt of a fire.
It was cut up and gone within an hour.
How many times I leaned against its length
waiting for the crossing light to change.

BILL'S HANGOVER

First thing in the morning first things: first light,
first sober notes of pigeons and some traffic, first
grays and pinnate shadows, first last blossoms of
ice just visible on glass, the window somehow open:
first voice in the head, clearing its throat, first
growl, first purgatorial pain, first one foot then
the other, debt paid out to debt, the body the money.
But first things first: a quantum taste of ash, a
thickness of the tongue too thick to swallow, first
breath almost warm enough to blur the first accounting
in the mirror: milk and honey of the eyes the wine
back into water, winter scouring of the skin pockmarked
with pimento, dizzy heights of childhood drawing blood,
the dark cardinal weight of the light heart doubled.

WHEN HE FELL BACKWARDS INTO HIS COFFIN

The rumor, because we all want to die happy,
is that he was in the bath listening to Verdi.
Probably singing, too, or mouthing with the masters.
So it must have hit him hard, the surprise faster
than a fall on ice or the missed step off a sidewalk,
his mouth opened wide in order to talk
himself out of it. The truth is he was resting
on the edge of an empty tub, fully dressed,
every cell, body and soul, beginning to annul
every future cell. And whatever he was thinking, solo,
a cappella, he must have had a moment,
as memory voided him, that he remembered, as he'd told it,
how his mother held his head down in the bath
to tease or test him, or both.

FOR JAN PALACH, A NAME DRAWN BY LOT,
ON THE ANNIVERSARY OF HIS DEATH
THE THIRD DAY AFTER ATTEMPTED
SELF-IMMOLATION IN PROTEST
OF COMMUNIST OCCUPATION
OF CZECHOSLOVAKIA,
JANUARY 19, 1969

I taught in your building once,
the one renamed for you
by the professors of philosophy,
a beautiful four-square block
of a building built to last centuries,
facing west into the hills backing
the great Vltava.

                    Afternoons
in class, looking across the river
through the wall-high windows,
I could see the thousand-year-old
crown of the Castle glittering,
and at night, standing on the Charles,
celestial above the city.

From here,
in the old ghetto, at the new century,
it looked benign, like a blessing
on your house and the half-dozen
synagogues and dozen blocks
of dwellings brought back to life
after your Cold War imitation

of the bonze priests in Vietnam,
who chose fighting fire with fire.
You almost died, then did, writing,
between life and death, that
I do not want anyone to imitate me.
The Soviets ignored you, though
they were mortal, too, in twenty years.

If I'd written your name with the poets
on the board, someone whose job it was
would've come along and erased it,
which is why pink marble and a plaque
were mounted at the entrance
of the building, whose former name
now no one can remember.

The Namesti,
the square that bears your name,
bore the names of soldiers
of the young Red Army—until nineteen
eighty-nine, the year no one had to die,
not God nor Kafka, for *whom the fire
to warm the icy world* was words.

AGAINST NARRATIVE

Hare, hunter, hound.
The sun rising the way it sets,
dark honey on the water, gold honey in the trees.
The day comes and goes, the novelist
lifts his pen, writes
from one side of the page to the other,
the happiness Alfred Hitchcock defined as a clear horizon.
The poet breaks the heart of that line.
Music, painting, poetry, all moving pictures
a movie that sits or rolls and spills, frame by frame,
a running time of, say, *The 39 Steps*,
each of the steps ascending or descending,
depending on Mr. Memory's memory,
under the spell of the faux Scots professor,
a master with the top joint of his little finger missing,
who would sell the secret to prewar Nazi Germany
four years before I'm born but loving this film,
Madeleine Carroll especially,
handcuffed to Robert Donat and dragged like a doll
through the Highlands in search of his murky innocence.
The long-dark-late-afternoon-into-the-night chase scenes
are, I think, the first film noir landscapes,
the high green tor moraine and worn shale-gray
half mountains and gorse-and-heather hillsides
disappearing into theater abstraction,
the low skies lit by sunset, then moonlight,

the Presbyterian town by candles at the corners:
broad visual realities finding subtle resolution
in the pure yet wifely face of Peggy Ashcroft,
also tied, in a different way, to a man,
Calvinist, farmer, and betrayer.
Beautiful women are, as always, cause
and effect—one dies, to start the plot,
one saves the star in order to continue it,
the third, the one we care about the most, is ambivalent.
And how quick they are, even the men,
how young on the screen these dead.
They move at the speed of intelligence and wit,
they appreciate the limits of their situation.
This is nineteen thirty-five, real time,
and if the secret reaches Hitler
the war will miss my birthday,
Sudetenland and Poland invaded years too early.
The story ends exactly where it started,
London's Palladian, with Memory back on stage.
"What are the thirty-nine steps?"
shouts Donat from the audience.

PASTORAL

Lee May's *Weeds* in April's *Attaché*,
starting with jimson and green dragon,
in isolated studies cast, Caravaggio-like,
against black space or high white
hint-of-blue, pictures of parts
of the plant perfected, thus exotic,
like nothing you'd see wild in the wild
side yard. A man wanted to catch a mouse,
but all he had was a picture of some cheese,
a joke to illustrate what's real versus
what we have to work with. Like wild
white indigo, everywhere a yardstick tall,
whose homeopathology is typhoid,
and whose young shoots in the spring
can be eaten as asparagus, but whose
piece-of-the-picture transformation,
at seven miles, thirty-seven thousand feet,
looks sterile, if inspired,
the two suspended testicle-sized pods
closed forever in the frame of their
abstraction. Sometimes, in order
to praise umbra, tone, and texture,
the way our best eyes praise purses of gold
in Rembrandt, tears in a Vermeer, rouged
Cezannean oranges, or evening geometries
in Klee, dead detail on an urn,

the sighting of a bird within its song,
sometimes, for kinds of beauty, you forgive
the beautiful, the photographic fragment,
the small and separate moment,
even a summer's sunset in a field,
your rough hand running the tops of thistle
and wild wheat, domed clusters,
and complexities of leaves,
the umbels, whorls, bracts, and involucres.

MEANDER

Yes, a river is a tree, a tree a river, built by source and branch-
ings,
like the river near Byzantium called *Maeander,* Byzantine with
tributaries
and blind offshoots, like that elm, closer to home, that earlier
every year
loses leaves, then towers in isolation, each divided limb finding
shape
inside the air, like this rain slip-slipping down the window,
capillary, fragmentary,
bled and bleeding out, a kind of river delta, spreading like the
root-like
veining of the heart or ganglia of nerve cells off the spine,
the spine itself a slight meander, rooted to the ground, branch-
ing to a cloud,
my heart, my spine, my cloud, the X-rays coldly spiritual, the
invisible made visible.
Of the six shapes in nature, the oval, the circle, and the hexa-
gon all close,
suggesting symmetry, endings as beginnings, the egg, the
moon, the perfect snow,
geometry and physics of completion, symbols of certainty, the
formal beauty of arrival.
That loving shape of the limb on the dying elm, how far from
where it started,
still growing, even now, toward ending, the way a river and its
runoff end.

OFF A SIDE ROAD NEAR STAUNTON

Some nothing afternoon, no one anywhere,
an early autumn stillness in the air,
the kind of empty day you fill by taking in
the full size of the valley and its layers leading
slowly to the Blue Ridge, the quality of country,
if you stand here long enough, you could stay
for, step into, the way a landscape, even on a wall,
pulls you in, one field at a time, pasture and fall
meadow, high above the harvest, perfect
to the tree line, then spirit clouds and intermittent
sunlit smoky rain riding the tops of the mountains,
though you could walk until it's dark and not reach those rains—
you could walk the rest of the day into the picture
and not know why, at any given moment, you're there.

THE WOMAN WHO SHOVELED THE SIDEWALK

She clearly needed more than money,
which, anyway, wasn't much.
Her dog, one of those outlawed fighting breeds,
black-and-white and eyes too far apart,
kept snapping at the leash, the cash
I placed as simply as I could into her open hand.
Her small stalled car was what she lived in,
the death seat and backseat all-purposed into piles.
She was desperate so she blessed me.
I could almost feel my mother standing there,
the way she'd greet the lost after the war.
A woman vulnerable is powerful.
Poverty in all the texts grants grace
to the raveled and unwashed,
just as the soul we assign to what is singing
in the trees, even in winter, lives
in the face and voice of the least.
You could see the random child in her,
who had got, today, this far.
You could hear, under her words, silence.
There wasn't that much snow, enough
to take its picture if you left it untouched.
Her companionable, hostile dog was what she had,
who stayed in the car while she started in earnest,
as if the work were wages. Young, off
or still on drugs—I couldn't tell—

she was alone in every hard detail.
Each day is lifted, then put back down.
Tomorrow's snow turns back into the rain.
I had to be somewhere but knew when
I got home she'd be gone. And the walk,
from start to finish, would be clean.

BIRDING

Some had the throats of sunsets,
some a pond's gray-blue, some had thumbnail necklaces,
some the white of paper or ink from the glass inkwell.
Then you had to cut them if only in order to count them,
there at the sunset, the still pond or the necklace,
the whistle of a voice whose windpipe was a reed.
If you were lucky the bullet would have passed
clean through the breast or lower, but we were
too young or inept to be that good or lucky.
The rule was a twenty-two, since a twelve-gauge
would leave nothing or various parts of nothing.
Most of the time we missed, so many points apiece,
though crows, the worst and largest, were worth double.
Birds were birds, and pests, especially in migration,
roosting beyond counting in the changing of the leaves.
Mr. Steinman, who had the no-neck look of an owl,
bald, broad, his horn-rimmed glasses round on his round
clock face, set on rounded shoulders, kept his own account.
We'd bring however few we had in burlap
and right in front of the class dump them on his desk,
whatever blood there was by now bled out of them.
Small bleak sparrows' heads and iridescent starlings',
wheat-brown tenor wrens' or easy mourning doves'.
And the blue crest or raven crown of a rare jay or crow,
sunlit at its brightest. The yellow-throated warblers'
and scarlet bandit cardinals' the sunset turning night.

FISHING DRUNK

One of the coolers filled with ice, the one
for fish, and one for beer and baloney,
and a bucket for bait that can be used
to keep some of the fish alive, the ones
we'll eat right off the campfire for supper.

At what point do we fall out of the boat?
The big, brindled pike, as long as I am,
lift their long faces up to look at us—
at least they seem to look, as we look down
into the dead black of water that has

eyes. Hours at the surface of a lake at
glacial depth. My uncle and my father
arguing nothing, then more pickerel,
elbow to the palm of the hand in length,
pulled in and hammered hard with a mallet.

Pickerel are dangerous, hook and knife.
My uncle, like those fishermen with guns,
shoots them in the head with bloodied fingers,
for which the full inebriated sun pours
down on him such light as to be blind,

so he sleeps off what little's left of the
stoned afternoon. My father finally, too.
We drift inside and outside of the light,
the tippler sun. I'm thinking we could die
out here, in the cold dark, in Canada.

SWEAT

Summer was worse but winter, too, the water seemed poured out of him, especially when the work squeezed hard enough to wring the heart out of the heart, the body glowing brighter in its oil. And the year he built the house, because it was a second, evening job, the beer with whiskey backs boiling from the massive forehead down, the big salt drops pooled off the nose like tears. Then those fluids we keep mostly to ourselves, that help us maintain balance or mean to make us lighter on our feet—the excrement, the urine, the violent black nosebleed, the serum semen phlegm we cough up in our sleep; blood on our hands, sun in our eyes; ichor, chyle and gleet, invisible, if painful, until some wound or hemorrhaging—my father refusing surgery from preternatural fear or superstition it would open up those secrets he wanted to take with him, *tempus in ultimum*, his to the end of time. But leaning into the heat of the rainbow he was welding or driving home a hammer on a nail, everything was obvious—the night sweats, stains, and last excretions, old terrors of the soul now almost cleansed; old memory, old worry, old matter from the softest tissue deep, upwelling from intestines and bad heart, emerging at the surfaces of skin, crude oil and water mixed, as if, by nature, he were fuel, combustible, on fire, the welder whose work it is to burn, the builder who dismantles, brick by board, his own ruined body in order to build.

SILENT HEART ATTACK

When silence is another kind of violence.
Like all the breath you've ever breathed
suddenly swallowed. But since it happened
over days, each night a little worse,
it lacked the drama of my father's death.
He went down, like a building, on his knees.
I sat in the dark inside the feeling
I was turning into stone, or, if I turned
around, to salt, salt crystals diamonding
the blackouts. Silence is what you hear,
the mouth a moon of o's, black filling up
the body with its blood. I listened.
Each night, all night, my father louder.

—The disciples out at sea again.
So many complications in the mission.
Five loaves and two small fishes
to feed the sick Tiberian five thousand,
who want to crown this miracle a king.
But Jesus will not suffer them their vanity
and leaves their lonely company to bread.
He finds another mountain: thus the twelve
abandoned, putting out to sea in the generalized
direction of Capernaum, lost without their master.
A storm blows up, the kind that makes of sailors
disciples of us all. Three, four miles,
twenty-five or thirty furlongs,
rowing in a wind that feels like crime.
They know they should have waited at the shore.
Fear, they know, is their faith tested.
Fear of the figure they now see walking toward them.

PASSERINE

That moment on the Campagna's "billowy wastes,"
a cardinal dressed like a cardinal,
accompanied by two footmen in bright livery,
shooting out of the sky songbirds.
"He had an owl tied loosely to a stick,
and a looking-glass annexed to move about
with every movement of the owl,
the light of which attracted numerous birds."
Severn adds it was astonishing the number.
Fowling pieces glittering with mirrors,
a burden of birds and "fragrances
and breaths from the distant seas."

Coleridge, the year before in Highgate,
complaining on a walk with dying Keats
of the noise of nightingales,
his and their insomnia,
their full vocative open-ended vowels
haloing what Milton calls the mournful
"liquid notes that close the eye of Day."
Shelley, on the Heath, listening in the dark
to the "Soul in secret hour"—
the skylark streaking back and forth
in song flight—"wherein we feel
there is some hidden want."

Wordsworth, quoting Bede, at Windermere,
that "Man's life is like a sparrow"
flying the length of a brilliant banquet hall,
"Safe from wintry tempest," ignored by king
and kind "Housed near a blazing fire."
The sparrow is "that transient Thing"
fluttering at the entrance
but now on "hasty wing," though from "what
world She came, what woe or weal/
On her departure waits, no tongue hath shown."
Not the trill tongue of the sparrow,
certainly, nor the wind,

out of the cold, that followed her—

HERMETICISM

The tiering up the hillside, the tearing up, too,
from so much sunlight, so much man-made beauty.
Marianna, Montale's sister, describes the family villa
as a sequence of gardens, multiples of trees,
and staircase after staircase climbing—masses of sage,
broom, and white and yellow flax, and palms mixed in
with poplars, holly oaks, (lemons), and candle-lit magnolias,
while higher up, placed between the olives and the pears,
valerian and cyclamen—then views of "little villages
grouped among the cliffs, hanging over the sea,"
the blue-eyed Mediterranean: all of it, to Montale,
imprisonment, a "counter-eloquence" of the mind at noon,
the sealed heart almost too deep for the sun. Summer's
language like sunlight on stone, light itself the stone.

TED HUGHES'S COLLECTED POEMS,

at some thirteen hundred and thirty-seven pages,
including notes and index, in the Farrar, Straus
and Giroux edition, is a tome, a tomb, too,
if you're a Hughes-hater, an omnium-gatherum
if you rejoice in the Lawrencian tradition of birds,
beasts and flowers. Then there's the aesthetic
dimension of the openness and violence of the verse
itself, if not exactly anti-English, pro-vers libre
in extremis, the integrity of the line interrupted,
challenged, as if with bare hands and a hunting knife.
Dead at sixty-eight, too young, Larkin at sixty-three,
of gin and loneliness and the stone chill daylight
of Hull, his *Collected*, in the old Faber and Faber
edition, a thousand fewer pages than Hughes's: who
became the Poet Laureate Larkin would have been
had he been different. Different the poems as well,
traditional as a tie on a librarian, if you go for
surfaces, but loving, unrelenting, savage underneath,
the slightly superior yet suffering tone discreet
as elegies, the rhymes the punctuation for what
cannot and can be said. *Now / Night comes on.*
                    Waves fold behind villages.

Lowell's *Collected*,
from the same publisher's hands as the Hughes, is larger,
if a hundred pages shorter, and this with prose,
appendices, revisions, notes, et al., while the F. S. & G.
American Larkin is more-as-less than the original.
Lowell, dead at sixty, dies in a cab, having flown
in from London and another life that day. What,
precisely, does a poem weigh versus all the poems
together? We read Lowell first, standing at the shelf,
and loved his energy, enjambments, and formal elegy
at the Quaker graveyard, even loved his esoterica
with God. Loved it when he changed and kept on
changing *Those blessèd structures, plot and rhyme—*.
We loved his madness, misalliance, endless notebook
sonnets. . . . Our own small weightless book, *The Dark*,
he gave a prize named for Delmore Schwartz is now
part of the air. The fear that the connection,
heavy in memoriam, might sentence a career was real:
dead at fifty-three, poet in his youth, paranoid
with promise, loved by friends regardless, lionized,
eulogized, remembered more or less, the worn-out book
of his body lay unclaimed for days in his last hotel,
                    In the naked bed, in Plato's cave.

"THE MORNING AMERICA CHANGED"

Happened in the afternoon at Villa Serbelloni.
We'd closed up shop on the work for the day
and decided to make the long descent down
the elegant stone switchback path into Bellagio
for coffee and biscotti. It was still Tuesday,
near a quarter to three, and a good quarter hour
to the exit gate, or if you stopped to look
at the snow on the Alps or at "the deepest
lake in all of Italy" or looked both ways
at once—as we say crossing a street—five,
ten minutes longer. This day was longer
because it was especially, if redundantly,
beautiful, with the snow shining and the lake
shining and the big white boats shining
with tourists from Tremezzo and Varenna.
And the herring gulls and swallows at different
layers, shining like mica in the mountain rock.
And the terra-cotta tiles of the village roofs
almost shining, almost close enough to touch.
Judith had already entered the pasticceria
and I was looking skyward on Via Garibaldi,
the one-way traffic lane circling the town,
when I heard the rain in the distance breaking
and then the voice through a window calling
and then on the tiny screen inside
pillars of fire pouring darkly into clouds.

LONG COMPANIONS

because man goeth to his long home

We are born the year Hitler invades Poland.
Blitzkreig, lightning war, war lightning.
We are three months old. And two-and-a-half
when Japan bombs Pearl Harbor. Kamikaze,
God wind. And six when the war is over,
all our uncles surviving in their uniforms,
our father head of the local National Guard
and responsible for German prisoners of war
our grandfather brings from Washington
to cut and plant Virginia. Some stay on.
After the war we move to far Ohio, where
Lindy Brubaker, prison camp survivor,
can't hold his food. He turns to God,
presiding, in fifty years, at our mother's
funeral, the girl who loves dancing, smoking,
and the movies. Shine Cinema, the Little Theater,
The Best Years of Our Lives, the Autry westerns.
Our father takes tickets to earn extra,
then comes home tight to Victory Heights
in order to rise, at dawn, to his real job
at French Oil. Like winter, Korea comes
and goes, McCarthy on TV alive and angry,
the moon drifting, the sun rising
on the multicolored back of the rooster, *fear*
the word of the day, Russia-China taking over,

their various massive hungers overwhelming.
Mongol, Manchurian, Manichean, Mississippian,
the black and white of cold war everywhere.
Gray pictures in the news, gray lives.
We are twenty-to-almost-through-our-teens,
and ready, in a steady year or two, to vote
for Kennedy, outlived by everyone, including
Johnson, Nixon, and the Cuban. And even
the Viet Cong, contraction of *Viet Nam Cong*
Sam, Uncle Sam, yellow peril nonpareil.
We survive our middle twenties thinking
purer thoughts and allowing the violent sixties
to become the virulent, violent seventies,
fingerprinted, visited, interrogated, inoculated.
Then we grow into a life of unintended consequences,
promises, spilled milk, The Great Wall
the Berlin Wall, any wall on which too much is written.
Tear them down, start over. Love our friends
anew, watch them disappear, one by one.
Watch the face of the deep darken
and roll in. Watch the tallest window
buildings break and fall. The heart bobs
and breaks. There is fire in the mirror,
a ghost peripheral profile at the eye.
Time passes, light pours, in themselves
                              a happiness.

GENE TIERNEY

I met her once in Houston in the eighties,
my mother's forties' idol and a woman
you could easily believe the most beautiful
on earth—a face, upon a time, to die for,
which recently her loved third husband had,
a real Texas oil-man and the opposite
of Oleg Cassini, the second or the first,
and a look-alike for dapper Clifton Webb,
whose character in *Laura* almost kills her.
The voice, like vodka poured through ice,
was gone, and the body, and the classic,
timeless face, all gone to weight, shock
treatments and commitments, pills, and
memory loss, gone with her depression.

It was a party—politics, Pick-Up Sticks
or worse, an art foundation fund-raiser.
She was the glamour and why we were there,
those of us who knew she's really dead
for only the first half of the picture,
then, suddenly, out of the rain, shows up.
It's her portrait and David Raksin's
music the audience falls in love with.
Yet meeting her I didn't think of *Laura*
nor her nominated role as the death-driven
wife watching the stricken polio victim drown.

It's in *The Ghost and Mrs. Muir* that her
1900 widowhood, her independent will, her
poignancy and beauty surprise the heart.

Now she's the one who'll love the dead,
and out of loneliness bring love back
through words and fantasy, as in a movie.
Now she's the one my mother wished she was.
The hero's Rex Harrison, sea captain
and a spirit, the setting the haunting
English coast, the Bernard Herrmann
score perfect for the heartbreak of how
time works its oceanic power. She ages,
Mrs. Muir, dies into love with just that
tragic edge Tierney brought to happiness.
At one point in the picture she's betrayed
by someone she thinks she's fallen for,
who isn't, in the end, the man of her dreams.

NOSTALGIA

Judging by the wingspan and particular pale
yellow, it had to be a swallowtail, a tiger,
judging by the stripes. It looped around me
several times, in and out of the flower beds,
in and out of the sunlight through the birches
and white ashes. It circled as if to warn me
of the bird I would have stepped on, a wren,
I think, gray as the asphalt.

                              "The natural
object is always the adequate symbol," though
Pound doesn't say if the symbol by itself is
adequate. The imagination makes from not up.
Which, in his recent essay on the subject,
"Reading Poetry," the critic Robert Scholes
seems sort of to agree with, that discovery
not invention is what brings the text to life.

He means the text of life as well. In his
argument he picks on all those Fugitives,
New Critics, and Elitists we read first,
those who chose John Keats and Yeats as
better, those for whom the art was sacred,
pure, those, like Cleanth Brooks, for whom
the poem was paradox, well-wrought. Scholes
is a democrat and thinks a poem is local,

thus finally user-friendly, and maybe, maybe
not—somewhere down the line—"symbol, tone,
and irony." Now, two thousand two, things
of course are worse, post-structural, post-
lyrical, post-Derrida and -Barthes, post-Paul
de Man, the Nazi, post-reading of the text,
while every other day is the birthday of poetry.
I remember, however, tiny Cleanth Brooks

reading, in the sixties, my first small book
in manuscript in front of me. He used a
magnifying glass, so as not, I thought, to miss
a word, and was dressed the way he read, elegant,
complete, blind to the irrelevant. Half-blind,
literally, at least. Yet he would certainly
have seen the bird grounded on one wing
before the butterfly; truth, then beauty.

JOHNSON HELICOPTERS INTO DAYTON

It's the summer the war comes home,
the summer the sixties become the sixties,
the summer *Time* declares Americans lack a tragic
sense of life, the summer Goldwater's the enemy—
reactionary, nuclear, ready to blow up social security.
Kennedy's been dead less than a year.
The electorate's angry, mostly gone.
My democratic mother, with me in tow, has seen
all the Trumans on the train, and Eisenhower and Mamie,
while Kennedy, alone, has passed these same downtown
streets royal in his limo, his young golden head
raised as on a coin into the open air of industrial Ohio.
Now Johnson, the Texan, terrible on television,
is live, having climbed out of the machine
into the distance above us, towering on the dais.
It's August and a quarter moon,
a scattershot, if that, of stars,
desultory buildings like a standing delegation.
He waves, he runs an arm across the crowd,
he speaks to us as if we were in school,
as if we're his Hill Country poor.
And we are in school and we are poor.
He's as tall as Lincoln, as committed as Roosevelt,
as ugly as Kennedy was beautiful.
That's his power, his nakedness in front of us,
his face in a fist, his real fist formed to hammer

on the dark. Only once does he mention his opponent,
only once Vietnam. The evil is poverty, ignorance,
Republican, them. He teases, he pleads, he y'all sings
moral conviction. Thousands, as thousands
tend to do, cheer, cry, and fill the infinite night dome
with love of what is lost the moment it occurs.
He's already president, he says, but needs reassurance.
Even better one on one, says the press. Lyndon
Johnson, body and soul—coonhound's ears,
surgery scars, bowel functions on the phone.
Tragic, loathed American.
When he lifts and flies back over us,
the searchlights off the copter are killing.

AUDUBON AVIARY

Aim and accuracy the silence
in the drawings, the stillborn
animation of the figures,
the mockers' static anger
at the rattler coiled to strike
the nest in what appears to be
a willow flowering yellow
at the stump end of the tree
bunched with the snake and birds
into a wild bouquet. . . . Songbirds
not the artist's habit—the serpent
introduced to elevate the scene—
preferring birds of prey
and the clean kill, peregrine
and red-tail, the singular osprey
and elegant black vultures, each
in the act of conquering the day,
while ornaments of parakeets
and passenger pale pigeons
and ruby-throated hummingbirds
here and there relieve intensity,
though in between the kite and hawk
and dove, three ignited blue jays
eat a songbird's swollen eggs, one
opening a shell, another drinking in
what falls, the third, in profile,

holding up an egg too big to break
or drop, stuck in its raven's mouth.
Audubon's style no less his prose
as a river journalist, his water route
his passage through America
and long descriptive passages
on birds, as if shooting
and painting weren't enough,
plus incidental writings on his
methods and an oddment simply called
"Myself." "I cannot help thinking
Mr Audubon has deceived you," Keats
writes his brother in Kentucky. . . .
"I cannot help thinking Mr Audubon
a dishonest man," who's sold George
Keats an interest in a boat
already lying on the bottom in the mud—
art, again, indifferent to the life
inventing it. To see alive a great
white heron in the stillness of its pose,
to watch a spectral whooper
lift into its dance, or a rare
snowy owl glide among the trees
is to almost miss the moment
and have to bring it back
diminished as a memory. The feathers,

the artist writes, are what inspire him,
by which he means a sort of texture,
but more than that the sheen,
the lightness and the color,
the way the light travels through
a thing, the way the water picks
the light apart, the feather oil
admixing all the waters. Nor
in his ode do we see the nightingale.
Nothing will hold the moment
save the kill. Audubon's silences,
his dark articulate stillnesses
are what we have against what
we'll remember. He shoots a fish
hawk, he writes, "at the Mouth
of the Big Miami . . . a handsome Male
in good Plumage. he was winged
only and in attempting to Seize
Joseph's hand, he ran One of his
Claws through the Lower Mandible . . .
and exhibited a very Ludicrous object."

SLOWING TO LOOK AT A DEER LYING IN THE GRASS NEAR AN ENTRANCE TO THE BELTWAY

Whole, as if, exhausted, it really has lain down,
clear of the roadside, tucked away from traffic.
No wounds, no trail of blood, no shadow animal,
no suicide, no star-point buck blinded with the scent,
no explosion into the headlights onto the windshield.
This one young, yet hundreds of dead weight pounds,
horns but barely horns, every inch a dreamer,
and if left alone tonight will wake and disappear,
the dreaming over, the way in sleep we all disappear
and wake to bodies of a piece, out of place. . . .
Of the family Cervidae, belonging to the order
Ruminantia, ruminators, contemplators, also known
as fliers for their ability to outleap sudden danger
and to sleep, at the ready, standing. Indivisible
from trees, the antler branching, vulnerable
to mirrors, arias, blue light across the lawns.

OLD DEBT

It acquires, like coral,
builds as easily and incrementally as gravity,
like climbing flights of stairs,
the higher the more history.
And whatever it bought and hasn't paid for,
it's different from bankruptcy
or borrowing against eternity,
and, like sin, more about the past
than the debit future—
time aging time,
like growing a glacier
or letting the leaves at the bottom of a pool,
era to dead era, pile, turn into coal and oil.
Nor will the millions the wealthy owe
help them pass through the blind eye of the needle,
since poverty is the original and natural state of things,
how we come into the world and how we should leave it.
The promissory note, the mortgage on the house,
the credit cards in multiples of gold,
the cost of living nickeled, dimed, deferred,
the heart attack or cancer,
a lifetime of the dailiness of days. . . .
My father in the bank, standing in the middle
of its open temple space,
silent as the looming Doric columns.
Nor will it end in the cloudy Attic afterlife,

among the silk and marble—
along the corridors, within the alcoves,
or leaning for the view from palace balconies,
some of us the emperors,
some the citizens now milling in the plaza,
dressed in shrouds with pockets or without.

AUTUMNAL

Not long before she died my mother told me
that her one regret was never to have traveled
and that since she had just read about it
or somewhere that reminded her from sometime
Venice was the place she would have gone to
and might still in her haunting of the afterlife.
She had already questioned God in heaven
and the heavy Bible verses she was taught
and now saw death as her last chance to live,
her last chance to spend the green-gold leaf
pressed into books each October on her birthday.
She wept, she understood the innocence of dying.
And here she was propped up against her pillow
the way she finally would be in her coffin
with her eyeglasses held between the light
and open page. She wanted me to hear the article
that said that Venice would be filled like all
Italy that season and that Venice in particular
was vulnerable and small, weighted with the souls
of travelers, and that in the Grand Canal
rivers of dark waters moved.—Would
there be space?—It said, *salotto citta*,
that Venice was a city the size of drawing rooms,
lit with the flowers of funerals and weddings.

MONOSTICHS

The iris in each eye is a flower, it sees as a flower sees.

Clusters, corollas, pinwheels, shapes in a far night sky.

Pointless to draw straight lines, to piece the dark together . . .

To gather fireflies, as in an open field tonight, hundreds.

Your new body now the several colors of the aster by the road.

There is pattern to these scatterings, if seen as a flower sees.

Your hand on my forehead at the pressure point of pain.

Nights I don't quite sleep, half dream through, I remember that.

Ashes from the chimney mixed with snow, dead leaves on the lawn.

The silver maple turning just enough to let the wind in, and rain.

In the window the full moon watching, thinking, making up its mind.

Summer or winter, the sky opens and closes, it is or isn't falling.

I'm alive because of you, I'm alive all night, and in the morning,

Like a penny's worth of fever, the sun is alive, burning down the dew.

EARLY AND LATE IN THE MONTH

Paddington Recreation Ground

1

White birds on the cold green winter grass, wet
with white, like snow held too long in the hand,
the runner's white breath ghosting the gray air.
The morning's one thing, then another—
rain, sometimes the sun slick along the trees,
sometimes the sudden thought of clouds settling
for the day, then lifting. While I slept none
of this was here, none of this drifting, though

I remember in the evening I watched
the sky hurt with the blue at the cold quick
of all color, then grow dark, and darker,
infinitely. The day moon held the moon.
I watched sunlight, hard against the windows,
disappear, watched the brickwork leave the dull-
red row of buildings, watched the street turn black
and electric, and finally oil with ice.

I woke up cold, like a boy late for school,
the photographic air granular, alive,
then lay almost an hour sorting nothing
from nothing, waiting for the room to fill.
Outside, in the half rain, half snow, half snow
themselves, the birds had gathered from the tide.
The man on the track was running away,
dressed in the cold colors of the morning.

First Day of Spring

2

All afternoon the industrial light
of London dissolving into rain,
the sexual, interminable patchwork
of the plane trees piling in perspective.
Silver and copper, like money in the street,
brilliant through the large upper window.
My eye, hooked like a bird's, fixes on
anything, even in memory: how the chill
rain washes clean, how the dry leaf opens
and is lifted back into the new wind.
The spirit puts its nose against the glass—
the sky is nothing, is a starved black wing.
Below: the mirror tops of cars, the warped
iron railing the kids will try to tightwalk.

GREENSBORO CAMPUS SONNET

Those seconds that the couple's kissing lasts,
an embarrassment of riches, so you look away,
then back, until by itself looking makes its
judgment: joy, then awkwardness, some sentence
in the mind interrupted. And the season
interrupted, from inward to this turning—
first crocuses and the lavender called redbud,
stunning girls with Walkmans wired and skating,
and heraldry of diamond shapes of birds against
the shielded, shielding brightness of the sky.
And old and loving rain thinking of starting,
whose scent is on the air, invisible flowering.
And yellow, then the red dress of the sun.
Love's cracked, healed-over cup full at the lip.

SAMUEL SCOTT'S *A SUNSET, WITH A VIEW OF NINE ELMS*

is,
at this distance,
from the other shore,
looking across the river north and east,
obscure about the kind of trees they are,
feathered in those other-century ideal humid greens
in a sort of flow toward the horizon and the ocean.
In perspective they diminish to depletion,
into the sunset's haw and haze,
as if the water had drained out of them into water,
though closer to the viewer they tower like clouds.
And this may or may not be Cuckold's Point—
the painter's put in buildings and boats
for reference and to tie the trees to work—
and the two men in the boat riding the drift
are either fishermen or journeymen,
one of whom is standing looking into the water,
while above his head,
where the dream Thames turns away,
is Saint Mary's Battersea.

DEDICATIONS

"Childhood"/Donald Justice, 1925–2004

"Against Narrative"/Howard Norman

"John 6:17"/Peter Davison, 1928–2004

"Passerine"/Michael Collier

"Hermeticism"/Harry Thomas

"'The Morning America Changed'"/Harry Berger

"Long Companions"/David Wyatt